SEX SECRETS

Deborah McKinlay gives advice on sex to 720,000 men every month. As well as being agony aunt for *Esquire* magazine, she is a bestselling author. She lives a long way from anywhere.

Also by the author

Love Lies
Bosom Buddies

Deborah McKinlay

SEX SECRETS

A Companion's Volume

HarperCollinsPublishers

This book is dedicated...
To a dear friend (who asked to remain nameless)
because she listens to all my stories, and tells me all of hers.
And... Tara Lawrence (who works terribly hard for my agent
Darley Anderson) because she is definitely a Good Sort.

HarperCollins*Publishers*
77–85 Fulham Palace Road,
Hammersmith, London W6 8JB

This paperback edition 1996
1 3 5 7 9 8 6 4 2

First published in Great Britain by
HarperCollins*Publishers* 1995

Copyright © Deborah McKinlay 1995
Illustrations by Josephine Sumner

Deborah McKinlay asserts the moral right to
be identified as the author of this work

ISBN 0 00 638801 9

Set in Berkley Book

Printed and bound in Great Britain by
Caledonian International Book Manufacturing Ltd, Glasgow

All rights reserved. No part of this publication may be
reproduced, stored in a retrieval system, or transmitted,
in any form or by any means, electronic, mechanical,
photocopying, recording or otherwise, without the prior
permission of the publishers.

This book is sold subject to the condition that it shall not,
by way of trade or otherwise, be lent, re-sold, hired out or
otherwise circulated without the publisher's prior consent
in any form of binding or cover other than that in which it
is published and without a similar condition including this
condition being imposed on the subsequent purchaser.

Contents

1	Taking The Plunge	1
2	Staying In Touch	6
3	Stale Mates	11
4	Good Vibrations	17
5	A Fly In The Ointment	21
6	Come Into My Parlour	26
7	Members Only	32
8	A Man In The Hand	36
9	Sticky Patch	41
10	A Moving Experience	47
11	T.L.C.	53
12	He Had It Coming	57
13	Missing Kinks	62
14	Playing Away	67
15	You'll Pay For This	72
16	Something's Up	77
17	Knock It Off	82
18	Sweaty Palms	88
19	Different Strokes	95
20	That Loving Feeling	101

At some point, when people are quite small and Much more interested in other things, Somebody big takes it into their head to say something like this to them:

'Boys are Different from Girls.'

If the small person is a Boy, the big person says a lot of other bumpſ and Then they say something like:

'You mustn't Hurt girls.'

If the small person is a Girl, the big person says Lots and Lots of other bumpſ and Then they say something like:

'You mustn't Trust boys.'

One day, when the Boy and Girl are all grown up,
the big Girl says to the big Boy:

'How could you *Hurt* me like this? I *Trusted* you.'

1

Taking The Plunge

....

When a woman goes out on her first date with a man she spends ages getting her hair to go right. She wears underwear which pushes some bits of her out and hold other bits of her in. She paints her nails and her face. She spends the entire evening pretending to be FASCINATED by moto-cross/futures/firearms.
Later, this woman accuses the man of having misled her.

....

Morning After Sickness is a female ailment. It affects those women who prefer to associate Sex with Romance. Single women over the age of twenty-five are particularly prone to it.

Sometimes women Frolic For Fun but often, if they wake up to find Love and Lust distinctly mutually exclusive, they feel Not their Best.

> Very few Modern Misses are emancipated enough to be completely comfortable, clambering from a cab at eight a.m., wearing . . .
> Last Night's Shoes.

A Man who wakes up with a bad bout of Wish You Weren't Here, just acts grumpy.

Sex Secrets

In the Olden Days, people Walked Out Together.
Then they Got Engaged and Then a gal said:

> 'Well, maybe...'

If they Didn't do this they pretended to.
Nowadays, nobody much bothers with these formalities.
Nowadays, most women are Won well before they are Wooed.
This wouldn't matter at all if Emotions were as easily shed as Wonderbras.
Unfortunately waves of confusion generally well up pretty soon after the underwear hits the deck.
Lots of women get caught in the Undertow.
Men just try to tread water.

The Modern Physical Romance goes something like this:
At some point a woman decides that she wouldn't object if a certain chap put his hand up her skirt.

Women say that they want men who are Nice with a Sense of Humour.
This is nonsense as lots of Nice men with a Sense of Humour can testify.
A woman wants a man who is Fanciable, and Nice with a Sense of Humour.

A woman helps a chap along by giving him some signals that she has reached the hand up the skirt decision.

THE SIGNALS

- Smiling a lot and tucking her hair behind her ear
- Laughing a lot and tucking her hair behind her ear
- Twiddling with something, tucking her hair behind her ear and doing that thing with her eyelashes.

Taking The Plunge

OTHER SIGNALS WHICH MEN SOMETIMES MISINTERPRET

Women . . .

- Dressing in the traditional style of streetwalkers
- Talking about hands going up skirts generally
- Taking off their skirts altogether

The thing is, men can be a bit slow to pick up on Signals so women need to give them the Go Ahead.

GIVING HIM THE GO AHEAD

Sometimes a woman who is fed up with waiting for a chap to Get the Hint surprises him by implying, in no uncertain terms, that he ought to *get on with it*.
She pounces.
A woman who is pouncing bears little resemblance to the coy, hair-tucking creature a man had supper with.
A woman who is pouncing is a passion machine, all flash undies and fingernails.
A chap usually catches on pretty damn quick and goes along for the ride.

In a first pounce situation there is a lot of fumbling. The woman is often wearing a complicated pre-pounce type of undergarment which the fellow can't quite get to grips with and this necessitates her removing it herself as part of the *get on with it* procedure.
It is quite likely that some items of clothing will remain on the bodies of the participants throughout a first pounce.
The woman loses an earring.

3

Sex Secrets

The whole affair is breathy and, often, reasonably speedy.
Names are avoided, as are Specific Requests.
A first pounce often takes place somewhere other than the bedroom. It usually leads there; via the bathroom.

The man

Goes to the bathroom to pee.

The woman

Goes to the bathroom to pee. She does a bit of a 'what do I look like?' inspection while she's about it.

If the first nighter is taking place at:

HIS place	**HER place**
The woman . . .	The man . . .
Is bemused by the magazine selection next to the loo. Feels a vague disquiet when she spots what looks like a woman's hairbrush on the shelf by the bath . . . Shrugs off the vague disquiet. Tidies all the bits of her that got untidied during the Pounce.	Wonders where she keeps the water glass. Once he has located it he puts it back anywhere other than where it was.

When the woman removes the last of her clothing and climbs into bed beside the man, she feels a bit shy and vulnerable. She gives him a shy and vulnerable smile. She wonders if he likes the way she looks.
She'd quite like him to tell her that he likes the way she looks.
Sometimes a man says something to a woman when he lifts the covers and indicates that she ought to slide over to him.
Usually this thing is either Sweet or Jocular. Usually this thing has nothing to do with the way the woman looks.

Taking The Plunge

Bachelor Boys often have their houses equipped with a few props for Get Lucky evenings.

Props:
- Alcohol
- A tape of pre-tested Seduction Music
- A candle

On a first-nighter the candle is for lighting. A chap can't always find the matches so he has to fiddle with the lamp for a bit instead.

The woman snuggles up to the man during this process. Sometimes a man responds to this snuggling in a very specific way. Quite often though, he simply smiles and slips contentedly, and remarkably swiftly, into the arms of Morpheus.

The woman lies awake for a while.

She hopes that she can find her earring.

She tries to remember when her period is due.

She feels a tiny bit In Love.

A small and almost imperceptible chant has started up somewhere in her brain. It goes like this:

> When will I see you again?
> When will I see you again?
> When will I see you again?

Mostly, women do not want to wake up with a man One Time Only.

If a woman wakes up with a man One Time Only she feels that she has been Won too easily.

This means that as soon as she wakes up with the man she starts to hope for a little Wooing.

If a man is accused of having given a woman a false impression with regard to Wooing he looks a bit surprised, he remembers the Pounce, he says:

> 'But it wasn't that kind of relationship At All.'

Mostly, women only understand One kind of relationship.

2

Staying In Touch

*****

'... that was about a week ago, what do you think?'
'Don't call him.'
'The thing is that he left a really sweet message.'
'DON'T call him.'
'And he might not know that I called back.'
'DON'T CALL HIM.'
'So wouldn't it be better if I did call ... just in case?'

*****

In the morning the man acts happy and cool. The woman tries to act happy and cool.

The problem for the woman is the Chant. Actually the Chant started before bedtime.

> **Lots of couples still follow the Dinner Date rule i.e. a chap is expected to shell out on scallops before getting his oats.**

A keen woman often finds that the Chant starts up somewhere between the middle of the main course and the pudding. While the man is telling her a fabulously amusing anecdote about his boss, she finds herself twiddling with her fork, smiling inanely and thinking:

>   'When will I see you again?'

(Sometimes this is quite a significant factor in the speed with which bedtime follows the pudding.)

Staying in Touch

If Any dates have preceded bedtime the man and the woman know some things about each other:

Things the woman knows:
- What the man's job is
- What car the man drives
- Where the man lives
- That the man has a cute way of eating peanuts
- That the man is potentially her ideal mate

Things the man knows:
- More or less where the woman lives
- More or less what the woman's job is
- That the woman is attractive
- That the woman has particularly attractive eyes/legs/breasts

Some couples still follow the Three Date rule.

An absolute pre-requisite for getting to third date status with a man is that the woman is not Boring. A man knows whether a woman is Boring before the main course on the First date and he is generally pretty pissed off about the damage to his Visa Card. Sometimes a woman will do three dates with a man she finds Excruciatingly Boring as long as *her* Visa Card gets to stay snugly in her handbag. This can cause a few misunderstandings at the point which the man considers to be post-third date bedtime. This man thinks that *après*-third date has been well and truly bought and paid for (the idea has sustained him through the damage to his Visa Card). He begins a spot of 'indicating his intentions' only to find himself Fobbed Off. Rather coolly.

In this situation a man cannot be completely relied upon not to punch the first thing at hand. Usually it is a wall. Sometimes it is not.

> No matter how many dates have preceded bedtime, a man and a woman tend to feel a bit shy with each other after a first night.

The man and woman have their breakfast together. The woman feels a little warm fuzzy feeling from knowing how he takes his coffee. She feels a little warm fuzzy feeling about Him. She would like to hold on to this warm fuzzy feeling forever.

Practical Considerations Intervene.

If they are at His place they get dressed and the man offers to drop her off somewhere.
If they are at Her place the man leaves while she is still looking appealing in a bath towel.

When the man leaves he looks into the woman's eyes. They kiss. She looks up at Him. He smiles at Her and he knows one of these things:

1. He is crazy for her
2. He has no intention of ever seeing her again
3. He is heading for deep trouble
4. He might take her to the party he's going to on Saturday night

No matter what he's thinking, he Says:

'I'll call you.'

The woman keeps smiling.
Inside her head the Chant begins to resemble more of a muffled scream.
Once the man has left she turns the radio up to drown it out.
She sings along to all the songs.
They make her smile. She is still smiling when she gets to work.

Staying in Touch

> When a woman gets to work after a First Night she looks all grinny and glowy.
> When a man gets to work after a First Night he looks a bit rough.

When the other girls notice the woman's grinny and glowiness they get a bit grinny and glowy themselves. They want to know ALL the DETAILS.
The woman tells them most of the details. There is a lot of laughing.
The woman keeps grinning and glowing till about lunchtime.
She hopes He will call.
At about three o'clock she feels a wee twinge of Morning After Sickness.
She shrugs it off. She hopes He will call.
By six o'clock her smile has developed a faint nervous twitch at the corners.

When the other blokes notice how rough the man is looking they like to say a few manly type things about it. These things are often very crude indeed. The man tells them to piss off. There is a lot of laughing.
The man gets on with his work.
At about six o'clock, when the man is feeling too rough to get much more done, he has a bit of a hunt for the piece of paper which has the woman's office phone number on it.

If the man has decided that he is
1) Crazy For The Woman
or
3) Heading for Deep Trouble
He figures that he may as well be hung for a sheep as a lamb and he puts the piece of paper somewhere where he can find it easily.

Sex Secrets

If the man has decided that he
2) Has no intention of ever seeing the woman again
or
4) Might take her to the party he's going to on Saturday
He figures he may as well hang on to the number and he puts the piece of paper somewhere where he is likely to find it in about three months' time. (At which point he might just give it another whirl.)

> A man only destroys a woman's phone number in extreme circumstances.
>
> These circumstances are: The woman woke up with . . . 'that look in her eye'
>
> Men know exactly what this look is.
>
> Women wish they did so that they could disguise it better.

Some men don't wait till six o'clock to call a woman they've spent the night with. Some men call her as soon as they've had a cup of coffee and fended off the other chaps.
Men who do this are either:

a) True-love romantic gems from heaven
or
b) Practised philanderers.

It takes about six months for a woman to figure out which.
She still gives him the benefit of the doubt.

3
Stale Mates

A woman goes home with a man. This man has two female flatmates. In the morning these women pound hard on the man's bedroom door. They laugh raucously. They shout:
'We KNOW you've got someone in there.'

A woman goes home with a man. She is a little Worse for Wear. In the morning she phones a friend. She says:
'Have you got an A to Z?'
'Yes, why?'
The woman leans perilously out of an upstairs window, then she says:
'Where is Acacia Avenue?'

A woman goes home with a man. She is Pretty Keen. In the morning the man says:
'What time is it?'
'Ten o'clock.'
'TEN O'CLOCK!!! I've got to be at the Church by eleven.'

Sometimes a woman meets a man and thinks:
   'What the Hell?'
A few hours later she thinks:
   'Where AM I?'

11

Sex Secrets

The woman keeps pretty quiet about this incident and then, one night, she thinks 'What the Hell?' and she tells some other women.
If these women are Good Sorts they laugh a lot and tell a few 'Where WAS I?' stories of their own.

Women's 'Where WAS I?' stories usually involve at least one of the following:

>   Alcohol
>   Christmas
>   An ex boss of theirs
>   The current husband of someone else
>   A mini cab

Women's *really*, gut-funny, 'Where WAS I?' stories (only told to other women who are Definitely Good Sorts) involve Menstruation.

Other things in the sexual arena which women Know are Hysterically Funny and men are completely in the dark about:

>   Poppers
>   Wonderbras
>   Anything to do with a Dutch cap, a tube of contraceptive jelly and one foot on a loo seat

Men suspect that women's *really*, gut-funny, 'Where WAS I?' stories are about Penis Size. They're wrong.
Women do not bother with whole stories about Penis Size. They either don't mention it at all, or they content themselves with throwaway comments which include the word 'Pencil'.
(Sometimes a woman merely lifts her hand and wiggles her little finger. Nothing more is said.)

Stale Mates

When women tell 'Where WAS I?' stories they are laughing at Themselves.

Sometimes, women can't see the funny side.
When a woman doesn't see her own role as comic, she is a lot less likely to tell the story at all.
If a woman Does tell a story in which her part is No Laughing Matter it's a 'Who Does He Think He *IS*?' story.

> A woman can Only see the funny side if she eventually reaches the conclusion that NEVER seeing a man again is probably a Good Thing.

Even if a woman wakes up with a man who is about to become her ex boss or someone else's husband, she still tends to take her time about deciding that never seeing the man again would probably be a Good Thing.
Usually, for a while at least, she clings vainly to the hope that a little Wooing might put things right.
This means that it is up to the man to do a runner.

All the time that a woman would, secretly, quite like to see a man again (if only to slap his face), she takes a Serious View of this behaviour.

Men tend not to tell 'Where *WAS* I?' stories.
Men tell 'Who was *SHE*?' stories.
Men use lots of words to describe the 'She's in these stories. Some of these words are very crude indeed. Usually, so are the stories.

When men tell 'Who was *SHE*?' stories they are Not laughing at Themselves.

Sex Secrets

When men set out with the Intention of finding themselves a 'Who was *SHE*?' story to add to their collection, they say things like:

'The perfect woman has great legs/tits/teeth and no last name.'

Men who are in this frame of mind are easy to spot. They look like wolves in wolves' clothing. They smell like aftershave and breath freshener.

Men who are in this frame of mind head for any place where they figure there will be a good supply of wine and women.

They spend an entire evening buying a gaggle of giggling girls an awful lot of drinks in the hope of going home with one of them.

This tactic is rarely successful. This tactic ranks with aftershave and breath freshener in terms of pulling power.

Men who *succeed* in the Instant Attraction stakes fall into two categories.

ONE
MEN WHO MAKE GROWN WOMEN SWOON

Often these men are pop stars. Sometimes they are movie stars. Sometimes they are men who can do magical things with sporting equipment. If a man who makes grown women swoon is Not famous, then he is certainly The Leader of The Pack.

A Woman who finds herself on the receiving end of a little attention from a Man who finds himself on the receiving end of a LOT of attention from women, is capable of forgetting where she is in a flash.

The man KNOWS this.

A man who makes grown women swoon finds pulling so easy that he is sometimes tempted to find out just how far a Swooner will go.

Some places that Swooners go

> Off their heads, with the help of illegal substances
> Onto the stage, minus some of their clothes
> Back to hotel rooms, with a large supporting cast

Some other places that Swooners go

> To court, with a flashy lawyer and a charge of statutory rape
> To the papers, with a whole wad of eight-by-ten glossies

TWO
MEN WHO JUST GET LUCKY

Getting Lucky accounts for the majority of Instant Attraction pulling.
Getting Lucky can happen to a chap who has never made anyone swoon in his life.
It happens like this.
A woman is at a party. She is bored witless. She has run out of her preferred brand of cigarettes. The friend she came with has run into some other friends.
This woman has had a few drinks, just to pass the time.
The next day she Can remember mooching a Camel Light from someone.
She Cannot remember how it was that, about four and a half minutes later, she was in an unfamiliar bedroom, with an unfamiliar man, on an unfamiliar bed which had a lot of unfamiliar coats on it.
Sometimes this woman is rescued by her friend.
Sometimes this woman gets into a cab with the unfamiliar man and snogs all the way to Acacia Avenue.
The man Cannot Believe how lucky he is getting.
He is pretty keen to *get on with it*, just in case his luck changes.
The man has had a few drinks too.
In these circumstances hands can get an awful long way up skirts before Acacia Avenue is even in sight.

Sex Secrets

In the morning the man . . .

Wakes up and sees what Mascara can do to a woman.
If he is a man who hasn't got lucky much in the past he is a bit shocked.
If he has played this game before he is a bit disgusted.
He acts off-hand.

In the morning the woman . . .

Wakes up and sees what a Hangover can do for a man.
It doesn't matter how many times she has seen this before, she wishes the ground would open up and swallow her.
She tries to act as if everything were perfectly OK.

Nobody mentions last names. In fact, first names are a bit of a blur.

The man, the woman, the friend, someone who went in for a coat and the cab driver have a new story to add to their collections.

'Where *WAS* I?', 'Who was *SHE*?' and 'Who Does He Think He *IS*?' stories have something in common.
They all involve easy Wins and absolutely no Wooing at all.

4

Good Vibrations

....

In spring, young women mostly think about:
Clothes

....

When a man Doesn't do a runner.
When a man calls a woman whom he has spent the night with, he is quite gooey to her. She tries not to be too gooey with him but, as the Chant fades, and her Morning After symptoms recede, she can feel her grinny and glowy mood taking over.
They decide not to see each other that night because they are both feeling pretty rough and they make a Date for Friday, Her place.

The woman

Tells at least one other woman about this plan. (Possibly tells several other women about this plan.) Spends a lot of time deciding What to Wear. (Discusses this with the other women.) Does something to her hair. Decides she isn't sure about what she's done to her hair. (Discusses this with the other women.) Has a person who dresses like a dentist, and inflicts about twice as much pain, do things to the hair on the rest of her. Buys some new kind of cream which makes thighs thin. Goes on some kind of thigh-thinning diet. Does something to her house which she saw in *Elle Decoration*. Buys a new bra. Has a last-minute change of heart about What to Wear.

Sex Secrets

The man pays very little attention to any of this on account of Passion and Desire.

The man has not bothered too much about his hair or clothes during the intervening days. This means that he has had plenty of time for musings on the Passion and Desire aspect of things. (It is not out of the question for a chap to have eased this situation slightly with the help of another woman. Women ignore this possibility.)

On Friday night, when the woman opens the door to the man, she smiles at him in a very welcoming way. He doesn't wait for her to Give Him the Go Ahead and they kiss for a long time on the landing. Eventually they pull apart, although the man still keeps hold of her hand. The woman uses her free hand to tuck her hair behind her ear and she smiles again at the man and asks him if he'd like a drink. Mostly a chap is prepared for this and has brought a little offering with him. Lots more smiling ensues. It's lovely.

Second Night Connection

On a Second Night a man and a woman feel as if they know each other very well. They feel that they have a bond on a Deep and Intimate level.
If they met in the pub two weeks ago, they are able to forget this fact.

The man and woman sit on the sofa. The man acts all familiar and puts his feet up on something. The woman likes this. She gets a good slug of warm fuzzy feelings while they are sipping their drinks.
They snuggle up. The man strokes the woman's upper arm in a way that implies he is thinking about stroking Something Else and the woman intertwines her legs with his. It is at this point that the man tells his first story.

Good Vibrations

> ### Men's Stories
>
> In the first weeks of a new relationship men like to ease the intensity of the atmosphere by telling a few stories. These stories are about themselves.
> These stories are about little quirky capers. The man is the hero in them but there are some minor characters. Childhood pets, boyhood chums and older brothers are favourites. Sometimes the other characters are women. The man generally avoids mentioning these women by name. This is because he is trying to be sensitive to the woman he is with.

The woman he is with couldn't give a fig.

A woman who is embarking on a Second Night has almost no grip of reality. She has lost touch with the world outside her sitting room. She is happy to listen to the man prattling on about Anything at All and she cannot (at this stage) imagine that another woman ever meant anything to him. This is because (at this stage) she KNOWS that no other man ever meant anything to her.

When the man has told a couple of stories and the woman has laughed in the right places, they look into each other's eyes.

> Women don't always realize that Laughing in the Right Places has an awful lot to do with sex.
> Women don't always realize that Men want Women who are Fanciable and Nice with a Sense of Humour.

They stop laughing. The stroking takes on a different sort of intensity.
The glasses get left somewhere perilous. Passion and Desire Intervene.

Sex Secrets

They go to bed.

The combination of Second Night Connection, story-telling, laughing in the right places and alcohol can have a spectacular effect on a man and woman in physical terms.
A few bridges have been crossed during the first night performance so the Second Night tends to be one of exploration.
Specific Requests may be hinted at. A lot of good times are had while the clues are laid.

At three a.m the man goes to find the glasses in the sitting room and the woman gets them something to eat.
She does a quick 'what do I look like?' inspection but she is a lot calmer about it. She feels so happy.
They eat the food sitting up in bed. They are very easy with each other. The covers are all crumpled and the man is awfully sweet and picks a pillow up off the floor for the woman to lean against. He thinks again what attractive eyes/legs/breasts she has and he may just tell her so.
The woman is delirious with happiness. The combination of this, the 'what do I look like?' inspection and Orgasm Afterglow can make her look pretty terrific. Her Looking so terrific can make the man Feel terrific. He tells another story.
This story ends in a similar way to the first. The glasses AND the plates are left somewhere perilous.

Much, MUCH later the man and woman fall asleep in each other's arms, unaware of the dawn light which is creeping in under the window shade.

The woman is quite a bit more In Love.
The man is Happy and Pretty Keen.

5

A Fly In The Ointment

....

'So I'd come in and they'd BOTH be there, yeah ... and they'd be really, you know ... getting it on ... but then they'd see me, and they'd stop, and they'd look at me and, you know, beckon for me to join them ... 'cos they'd be BEGGING for it, right ...'

....

Wonderful Second Nights often lead fairly smartly into third, fourth and fifth nights. These become a blur of candle wax, long baths and three a.m. food consumption. The man and woman do not like to be apart. When they Have to be apart they have an awful lot of telephone conversations. These telephone conversations would sound very silly indeed to anyone else.

N.B. Modern Women DO NOT go around talking about being In Love.
They don't have to because the other girls do it for them.
As the grinny and glowiness intensifies the other girls say lots of things like:
'No use asking her. She's IN LOVE.'
There is a lot of laughing.

Sex Secrets

> Modern men (or any others for that matter) *definitely* don't talk about being In Love. After a while the other chaps catch on though and they stop being quite so crude about how rough he looks in the mornings. They don't laugh as much.

When the woman is well and truly hooked and the man is feeling at his roughest, Real Life intervenes. The Overlap Issue pops up.

THE OVERLAP ISSUE

Women tend to avoid Overlaps.
Either: They take a good long while to recover from the ending of one relationship before embarking on another
Or: They like to make a clean breast of it to the Overlappees pretty early on (about five minutes of nail-biting, tears and general angst follows) and then throw themselves wholeheartedly into the new relationship.

Women still believe in the concept of One and Only.

Men are more cautious.
Men's cautiousness gets them into some real scrapes with women.
The Tandem Scrape is the most common.

When a single man meets a new woman it does not matter how fabulous he thinks she is, it does not matter how wonderful their nights of passion are, it does not matter how often he finds himself phoning her about something very trivial indeed.

HE DOES NOT THROW AWAY HIS INVENTORY.

Sometimes this Inventory has already been eroded somewhat. Sometimes this Inventory has been whittled right down to ... ONE. (Men never really like to face up to this idea.)

A Fly In The Ointment

When a man's Inventory is down to One and he decides to make it Plus One his life gets a bit complicated. He puts these complications to the back of his mind for as long as possible.

One night the woman makes the bold move of suggesting that they do something (it doesn't matter what this something is) on the weekend.
She suggests this while they are eating bacon sandwiches in the bath at two in the morning.
Silence.
The man wriggles, just slightly, but enough to splash her sandwich.
The woman knows that her Happy Bubble has sprung a leak.
She loses her appetite. She puts the damp sandwich down on the edge of the bath and slithers around to face her dream man. She strokes his chest and looks up at him as seductively as she can manage with the hiss of escaping air in her ears.
She says, 'I just thought . . . ' She plants a soft kiss on his nipple.
The man wriggles again.

Hissssss

The man pushes her away, very gently, very firmly. He gets out of the bath and wraps a towel around his waist. He has his back to the woman when he says:
'It's Jen's birthday on Saturday.'

BANG

The enormous and overwhelming implications of these five words are too much for the woman to take in at first. She doesn't speak.
The man leaves the bathroom.
When the woman comes out of the bathroom (her eyes have the expression of someone who has just survived a serious car accident), the man she sees sitting on the bed looks different to her. He looks like a strange cold person whom she hardly knows.
She says, 'You're still seeing her?'

Sex Secrets

Her voice is very quiet and has a shaky edge to it which melts the Ice Man a little bit.

He says, 'Look, I promised. It's just this weekend. It's her Birthday.'

The woman still looks like a deer in his headlights, he softens some more, he puts his arms around her, ever so gently.

He says, 'I'm sorry, sweetheart, we'll do something next weekend . . . huh?'

The woman doesn't speak.

The man takes this as a sign of assent and, keen to avoid further conversation, begins their usual after-bath, two thirty a.m. routine.

The woman does not stop him but a little bit of her goes cold. A little bit of her that was His before is denied him now.

Sometimes, when one bit of a woman goes a bit cold, another bit of her heats right up.

This means that an Upset and In Love woman might eschew lovey-dovey love-making in favour of a more fiery variety.

Billing and Cooing goes right out the window. Biting and Scratching comes in.

A man is not averse to the odd throw of passion but a change in routine can confuse him.

The man senses that things are Not what they were. He feels a bit angry inside. He feels a bit angry at both the women for getting him into this scrape.

(Later, when he goes for a pee and catches sight of his left shoulder in the mirror, he is likely to feel thoroughly pissed off about the Biting and Scratching.)

At breakfast Tears are in the Air.

When a man figures that Tears are in the Air . . . he often makes the mistake of trying the Jocular approach first.

A Fly In The Ointment

It doesn't work.
He tries acting Sweet.
That doesn't work either
When a man (who is in the wrong) starts acting Sweet to a woman (who is near to tears), the woman senses her advantage. She gives him the Cold Shoulder.

Once the man has left, the Cold Shoulder shudders and Tears are all over the kitchen table.

6

Come Into My Parlour

'She should have hung in, he was going down.'
'What do you mean Going Down?'
'Well . . . he might have married her.'

'She really got him.'
'How do you mean Got Him?'
'Well . . . he couldn't get out of it could he?'

One of the speakers is a Man.

A woman who is seeing a man who is seeing another woman Has Her Suspicions.

Item One:
The man has only called her once in ten days (twenty-four tell-tale hours after her call to him.)

Item Two:
He is being Off-Hand and Noncommittal about her Birthday.

Come Into My Parlour

> When a man is talking to a woman who Has Her Suspicions, he feels a scrape coming on. His voice takes on a similar tone to the one which he uses when dealing with the dentist's receptionist.
> This is true whether he has known the woman for five weeks or fifteen years.

A woman who finds herself on the receiving end of this tone senses Impending Doom. She tries to remind herself that this man has told her that she is Wonderful and Sexy and Fabulous. She tries to conjure a mental picture of him brushing his teeth in the nude.
It's no good.
She finds herself behaving like a dentist's receptionist.

'What time then?'. . . 'Well, I hope you'll call this time and not just leave me waiting.'

A woman who Has Her Suspicions KNOWS that behaving like a dentist's receptionist is Not the best course.
It's no good.

She says something like:
'But you'll DEFINITELY be here on Saturday, won't you . . . WON'T YOU. It's MY BIRTHDAY'
The man (who is seeing another woman) says:
'I   Said   I   Would . . . all   right?'
He figures that Tears are in the Air. After he hangs up he thinks: 'Oh hell, I've got to see her on her Birthday. I will, I'll see her on her Birthday . . . definitely.'

Once the man has made this decision he feels his guilt lift somewhat. He feels quite a bit better actually. He ignores the nagging twinge that is asking him HOW he is going to get this past the new woman. He figures that things will work out, somehow.

Sex Secrets

By Friday morning Nothing is going well for the man.
The New Woman is giving him the Cold Shoulder.
The woman who H.H.S. has left a whiny Birthday reminder on his answer machine.
(If the man notices a few Biting and Scratching reminders when he is shaving, his mood turns really nasty.)

When some fool from the foreign desk makes a smart-ass remark about the on-goingness of his Bit Rough state the man makes it damn clear to him that he should keep his mouth shut.

On Saturday though, the man is feeling more himself. His left shoulder is pretty much restored to its former glory. He manages a trip downtown to buy a birthday present. (He plans on a bit of a scout for a new CD player while he is about it.) He gives the gift-wrapping girl at the perfume counter his cheekiest smile, just to perk himself up, and when she smiles back he feels his usual *joie de vivre* restored.

Men Flirting Madly

Often, men flirt with women just to remind themselves that they could pull if they wanted to.
Fanciable women are meant to flirt back.
Unfanciable women should just act grateful.
There are two responses which Really put men off their stride when they are flirting for fun:

1 An unfanciable woman who says:
   'In your *DREAMS*.'

(Afterwards the man consoles himself with the idea that this woman's sexual tendencies are not of the hetero variety.)

2 A fanciable woman who says:
   'Drop 'em right here, big boy. Let's see what you're made of.'

(Afterwards the man consoles himself with the idea that he could have if he'd wanted to.)

Come Into My Parlour

Now, this perfume that the man has bought is bloody expensive, Plus he has splashed out on some other stuff that the smiley girl suggested, so he really can't imagine that anything can go wrong.

Secretly, men never feel that they get quite enough Praise and Recognition for the amazing feat of Buying Women Presents.

The man spends a pleasant afternoon tinkering with his new CD player.
Things will work out.

The woman who H.H.S. spends the day in a quandary. She cannot decide whether Confrontation or Conciliation is the best policy. Her friends cannot agree on this either. The only thing they all agree on is that she should look pretty Hot when the man arrives. This takes quite a lot of time to achieve because of the crying-night's puffy eyes. But she manages it.
The evening goes like this:

> ***The woman who H.H.S.*** opens the door to the man, she smiles at him in a very welcoming way (she has decided on Conciliation). She kisses him for a long time on the landing.
> (***The new woman*** puts on a face mask.)

The man pulls away, ever so gently.

> ***The woman who H.H.S*** keeps hold of the man's hand. She tucks her hair behind her ear with her free hand and asks him if he'd like a drink. She smiles.
> (***The new woman*** puts on a calf-length terry towelling robe. It's a bit faded.)

The man notices that the woman who H.H.S. is wearing a Hot-looking black outfit. It's a bit tight. He tries to put this to the back of his mind. He goes into the sitting room and sits on the sofa.

Sex Secrets

>***The woman who H.H.S.*** pours a couple of drinks.
>She makes sure that the man gets a good eyeful of
>the most spectacular angle of the Hot-looking black
>outfit when she hands him his glass. Then she
>snuggles up next to him on the sofa.
>(***The new woman*** switches on the telly.)

The man doesn't put his feet up on the coffee table
the way he usually does.
The thing is, the man is feeling a touch uneasy.
He sips his drink, thoughtfully, for a moment.
You see, he hadn't planned on this.
He'd planned on a pleasant enough, straight
forward kind of evening. An evening of making
it clear that he is a very nice guy who doesn't hurt
people. Followed by a bit of a disappearing trick.
(He doesn't really admit this last bit to himself but
it is true.)
He had not planned . . . well. . . he'd had something a little more sedate in mind.

>***The woman who H.H.S.*** strokes the man's arm in
>a way that implies she is thinking about stroking
>Something Else. She twiddles with the stem of her
>glass. She does that thing with her eyelashes and
>Then she says:
>'I thought we'd have dinner here, darling. I've
>cooked something special.'
>(***The new woman*** starts to cry. Cracks appear in
>her face mask.)

The man knows that he is 3) heading for very
deep trouble indeed.

Bottom Line

Fully grown fellows are capable of completely losing sight of the
concept of Free Will, when they are dealing with women.

Come Into My Parlour

They pretty much feel that they are In The Woman's Hands.
They pretty much feel that they are Not Really accountable for their actions.

If a woman goes for the direct approach, puts her glass down somewhere perilous and slides to her knees in front of a man . . . The man feels that he is Not At All accountable for his actions.

7

Members Only

....

'So, she leans over to get the popcorn out of his lap and ... he's ... you know ... got a ...'
'NO ...'
'YES ...'
'How hysterical.'

Willy, Wopper, King Kong, The Bishop, Love Muscle, Joy Stick, Ram Rod, Old Reliable, Big Boy...

Women, name their cars.

....

When a man finds himself heading for Trouble of the woman sort, he gets to thinking.
He thinks about a Womanless Life.
In a Womanless Life a man wouldn't have to Lie.

Men don't actually Want to lie to women. They just don't want to have to Tell them anything.

In a Womanless Life, there'd be no sticky questions, requiring yes or no answers, like: 'Are you still seeing *Her*?'

Members Only

A Womanless Life would have other advantages too.
In a Womanless Life, Impressing people would be a much more straightforward business.
In a Womanless Life, Impressing people would Not involve Scallops and Visa Cards.

A man can really work himself up to this theme.

If a man could live a Womanless Life in a Womanless house he could have things exactly as He wanted them. No nonsense. No knick-knacks.
Nobody would Ever say: 'Aren't you going to shave?'

There is another reason that a man can imagine a Womanless Life so well.
It's This: a man already has a Love Object of his very own.
This Love Object is with him All The Time.
This Love Object has been with him ever since someone big said:

'It's a Boy!'

One day, when a boy is just a bitty baby, his teeny-tiny Love Object stands right up and says 'how do you do?'
Often the only witness to this brazen display is the bitty baby's mum.
She laughs like a drain.

One day, when a boy is a wee bit bigger, his mummy tugs his trousers down in the park. She points his itsy-witsy Love Object at a tree and tells him to pee.
A sweet old lady walks past and laughs like a drain.

After a while, boys get a bit wary of mums and old ladies, and anyone else who uses the words 'Winkle' or 'Tinkle'. Boys decide to keep anything to do with Winkles and Tinkles to themselves.
It's about this time that the Special Relationship really begins to develop.
It develops at every opportunity actually.

Sex Secrets

Mums, old ladies, and the entire Winkle-and-Tinkle brigade say: 'He'll grow out of it.'
They say this when the boy is rolling on to his stomach at the swimming pool.
The girls at the swimming pool go into the changing rooms and laugh like drains.

The Special Relationship between a boy and his Love Object is a mutual affair.
The Love Object is the first to introduce himself but the boy wastes no time in shaking hands.

One day, when the boy is Big, he meets a woman who seems to Appreciate this.
When this woman laughs like a drain it isn't in a Winkle-ish or Tinkle-ish kind of way. Another Special Relationship develops.
The thing is, you can't expect a fellow to forget an old friend, just because a woman has entered the picture, can you?
A chap still likes to say hello occasionally.
A Modern Woman Knows that a man might resume this relationship every now and then:
She thinks that a man does this because SHE is not about.

The truth is that a chap does this because:

> She is not about
> Nobody else is about
> Just because

Sometimes a woman realizes that SHE is not a man's only source of pleasure. Quite often this is because she has run across something which provides her with Concrete Evidence of this fact.
She assumes this something is a Substitute for Her.
Sometimes this woman waves this something at the man and gives him a right Telling Off.
Sometimes she doesn't say a word.
Sometimes she tells this story to a few friends and they all laugh like drains about it.

Members Only

In a Womanless Life a Man would Not be an Object of Mirth.

Men discuss the Womanless Life thing with each other.
(Quite often men talk to each other in a way that would get them a right Telling Off if they did it in front of women.)
Unfortunately for men, they don't talk to each other about very much else.
Sports, of course, and Cars are Guy Things but mostly a Chap doesn't Chat.
Mostly men get together to Do stuff to other Stuff.
Mostly a Man who wants to really bare his soul would like to do so with his head in the lap of a Woman.
In fact a Woman's Lap holds a whole bevy of attractions.

There are men who are happy doing lots of things with their heads in the lap of another man. These men manage a Womanless Life but they still have someone asking them when they're going to shave.

Lots of men find that just as they are about to sign up for a life of eating baked beans and ice cream, straight out of the packet, The Woman's Lap Attraction gets them.

Somehow, no matter how clever men are about substitutions for Women's Laps, a Live One retains its allure.

When this lap is attached to someone Fanciable and Nice with a Sense of Humour the man finds himself shaving and showering and dusting off his Visa Card quicker than you can say, 'I'll call you'.

8

A Man In The Hand

'So, in the morning, he mentions this party that he might be going to and then he says he'll call me . . . that was two weeks ago . . .'

A man considers a woman to be his EX girlfriend long before the woman in question is aware of this fact.
A man does Not admit that sleeping with a woman who he considers to be his EX girlfriend might add to this confusion.
A man Is vaguely aware that the woman who he considers to be his current girlfriend Might Not see things this way.

> Men Dream of Clean Getaways
> Life and Women conspire to Deny them the
> realization of this dream

The man senses that the wee birthday celebration has failed to extricate him from the Tandem Scrape. He figures that lying low for a bit is the best policy.
It is.

Men's Lying Low Tactics
Not calling

Women's response to Men Not Calling
No Call Neurosis

Women who are toying with the idea of ditching a man who is seeing another woman have their Ditching Speech all prepared. They plan to give it to him Straight. Just as soon as he calls.
He doesn't.

The woman who has put All her energy into getting a man back under her duvet and Succeeded says:
'If only I hadn't SLEPT with him.'

The woman who has spent several miserable Nights In dreaming of having a man back under her duvet says:
'As long as he didn't SLEEP with her . . .'

Not Sleeping With Her . . .

Women say:
'Well they still see each other/live together/are married but –
they haven't Slept Together for years.'
When a man, whom a woman Loves, gives her the old Don't sleep together line, she believes him.
But then . . .
Men believe that none of the women *They've* slept with have faked it.

Sex Secrets

Once the woman who the man, more or less, considers to be his current girlfriend, has convinced herself (and anyone else who will listen) that:

He Didn't Sleep With Her

she pops out to Paperchase at lunchtime. She buys a card with a Perfect 'just us' message on it. After lunch she bikes this card to the man's office.

When a man, who is having an otherwise irritating day, receives a 'just us' message from a woman he is Pretty Keen on, he feels good. He calls her.

> **N.B. This reaction is dependent on the Pretty Keen part. If a woman who a man considers to be his EX tries this trick she is liable to find herself suffering a double dose of No Call Neurosis with lots of Morning After Sickness thrown in.**

Reconciliation Calls are of the gooey variety.

The woman . . .
- Thinks that this call marks a New Beginning in the relationship
- Assumes that the man will Never see his EX again.

The man . . .
- Thinks that he is off the hook.
- Assumes nothing of the kind.

A note about New Beginnings

> **Women have a remarkable ability to blot out the anxious and unhappy bits which precede New Beginnings. Women are able to forget the pain of child birth when they hold their babies for the first time.**

A man cares about his EX. (*THAT's* why he sleeps with her if she acts like she wants him to.)

A Man In The Hand

Sleeping With Her If She Acts Like She Wants Him To...

Most men don't Want to hurt women.
Most men figure that Rejecting a woman will hurt her.
Very few men stop to think about the consequences of saying Yes to a woman and then Ignoring her for the rest of her life.

BUT once a man has a new woman pretty much in tow, he figures that life will be a lot simpler if he gives his EX a Wide Berth for a bit.

GIVING HER A WIDE BERTH FOR A BIT, THE FACTS:

Generally men do not Leave women. They just give them a Wide Berth for a bit.

Men reckon that they can give a woman a Wide Berth for a bit and then, if they feel like it, they can give it another whirl.

A man who has given a woman a Wide Berth for a bit (any period up to three years) is perfectly capable of suddenly phoning this woman and chatting to her as if they were in the supermarket together only yesterday.

Sometimes, while the man is giving the woman a Wide Berth (and the woman is having a nervous breakdown and doing her best to obliterate all traces of him from her life) he decides that he is, after all, Pretty Keen on her. He decides that he might just give her a call any day now and get things rolling fairly seriously.

He is genuinely surprised if the woman shows no interest in complying with this plan.

Sex Secrets

Sometimes a man Does decide to Leave a woman.
Usually this is because the woman has Not respected the fact that he is trying to give her a Wide Berth for a bit.

A man tells a woman that he is going to Leave her by telling her that he is: going to give her a Wide Berth for a bit.

9

Sticky Patch

A man can say 'It didn't mean anything' and Mean it.

A man can say 'Uh-huh' and not mean anything at all
'I said to Carol that we'd definitely be going on the skiing trip next February.'
'Uh-huh.'

'I thought it would be nice to spend Christmas here, so I told Mum that they were welcome to come to us.'
'Uh-huh.'

'I'm sure it's the Pill that's making me put on all this weight . . . I think I should go off it for a while.'
'Uh-huh.'

A Pretty Keen man who has allowed his Inventory to slide back to low, single digits often feels the need to consolidate his situation.
At this point the man and the woman begin to play the game in earnest.
The man sends the woman a 'just us' message.
(They both consider that this single effort is equal to all of hers put together.)

Sex Secrets

A man's 'just us' message is usually read by several women, other than the one it was sent to. Many a male-sent 'just us' message is left idly on a desk or mantlepiece so that even casual passers-by can have a good shufti.

A man and a woman who are not seeing any other men or women, and who are seeing rather a lot of each other, are liable to give in to their gooey feelings.
The addition of Love Stuff to a relationship usually results in a Lot of Love-making.
Early days love-making doesn't require much along the Associated Props lines.
Early days love-making is more along the get your gear off, any time, anywhere and almost all of every night lines.

When it comes to In Love love stuff:
Men want to do it more   Women want to do more of it
Mostly nobody bothers much with the distinction. Everybody is having too good a time.

This good time could go on and on if the woman didn't start Listening too hard.
She is listening for Terms of Endearment.

A woman
Wants to hear that she is loved, beautiful, the best, beautiful and loved. She wants to hear this a lot.

A man
Thinks that if he has told a woman he loves her in the morning, she will assume that this is still the case in the evening.

A woman
Would like to hear a few Terms of Endearment when she is in bed with her beloved.

A man
Who is moved to speak when he is in bed with his beloved often says something which could not be classified as a Term of Endearment.

Sticky Patch

Lots of women complain about Men's lack of ability to Talk in Bed generally.

These women have never watched a man try to answer a question and back out of a parking space at the same time.

Men just complain about women Talking, full-stop.

When a woman feels that she is Not getting enough in the Terms of Endearment department, she gets a bit tetchy. She gets a bit concerned.
At first she allays her anxiety.
Not for long.
One night (when she is in bed with her beloved) she says:
'Talk to me.'
This is man's cue for an awful lot of Terms of Endearment.
(Most women wouldn't mind a bit of sauce on top.)
Men don't always pick up on this cue.
Generally they:

a) Keep moving right along with no verbal response whatsoever
b) Mutter something incoherent and then keep moving right along
c) Think that this is a chance for a Specific Request and say a sentence with the word (or words pertaining to) 'Bottom' in it

Any of the above can set off a Post-coital Huff.

Sometimes a woman gives a chap one last chance to allay a Post-coital Huff.
She waits till things have slowed up. She waits till the duvet cover is on the floor. She gazes, doe-eyed, at the man (who Still shows no sign whatsoever of Speaking) and Then she says:

'What are you thinking?'

A man does not like this. He does not like this one bit.

Sex Secrets

He does one of these things:
- Nothing
- Attempts a response

He is unlikely to be on to a winner with either of these.

A woman who has asked 'What are you thinking?' at a time like this Already has a Huff coming on.
Unless a man is prepared to lavish her with an awful lot of Terms of Endearment, for what seems to him like an Interminable length of time,
The Huff will out.
Mostly, men would just like to go to sleep.

POST-COITAL HUFF SYMPTOMS IN WOMEN

- Pouting
- Moving right to the edge of the bed (back to the man)
- Sighing
- Going to pee and not rushing back to bed (taking ages, actually)
- Smoking

Men are oblivious to all of this behaviour. If they notice any of it they ignore it. Women try it anyway.

If a woman is at His place and he is ignoring her Post-coital Huff she is liable to really go into one.
She packs all her stuff. (Well almost, she leaves her hairbrush in the bathroom.)
Then (when the man *really* can't pretend to Still be asleep) she goes back to Her place (Well, she Threatens to at least.)
The man does not understand how this happened.
This is how it happened.

Sticky Patch

Woman's Version

He met me after work at the usual corner. I was really looking forward to seeing him and gave him a huge kiss. He wasn't very responsive. He said the lights were changing and we'd better hurry. I felt a bit upset, but I tried not to show it. I suggested that we go to Luigi's which is Our restaurant. He said OK but he was still in a funny mood. When we got to Luigi's, I tried to cheer him up. I told him Carol's funny story about the parking spaces. He smiled a bit at that and then he asked me if I thought he should have lamb or pasta. I said pasta was better for you but he should have lamb if he felt like it. He ordered lamb. He ordered a bottle of that Chianti that we always have and he seemed to be more relaxed when we were eating. I told him about the holiday brochures but he didn't seem all that keen so I just asked him how his lamb was and he said 'Not bad' and I asked him how work was and he just frowned so I shut up and smiled and said 'Ready to go then?' and we got the bill. We played Our tape in the car on the way back to his place and we both sang along. He took my hand and kissed it while he was driving which I thought was really sweet. When we got out of the car I said 'I love you' and he kissed me. As soon as we got inside he started kissing me again . . . next thing we were on the bed, half undressed making love. He seemed sort of detached though. And then afterwards he was all distant and quiet. So I gave him a little hug and said 'Is something the matter?' and he said 'No', just like that, and nothing else, and I said 'Well obviously Something is, you've hardly said a word all evening,' and he said 'Just come to bed, huh?' which really irritated me. Sometimes I feel as though he shuts me out. I wish he'd Tell me what he's feeling. I mean we spend the whole evening together and he hardly speaks and then it's Bonk and Bed. I went into the bathroom and sat on the edge of the bath thinking about it all and I thought, you know, I don't want this. I want someone who I can feel relaxed with and I just thought I'd much rather be at my own flat in my own bed. If all he wants is sex then he's had it and I decided to just go home. I noticed that I had a spot starting on my chin too which *really* annoyed me.

Man's Version

Shitty day. OK meal. Great sex.

It is hard for the man to make the connection between His version, and a fully dressed, sulking woman who is calling a cab at midnight.

10

A Moving Experience

....

'Heaven knows what the chamber maid thought . . .'

'Heaven knows what the customs man thought . . .'

'Heaven knows what the neighbours think . . .'

....

Mostly, men have three basic motivations for any action:

1. It feels good
2. It enhances their status in some way (i.e. Power or Money)
3. It might get them out of trouble

There is one particularly powerful motivation to which men are not subject.
Women are. It is:

1. What do other women think?

Women deny this but it is true.

The other women ask the woman how things are Going with the man.
They ask this rather a lot.

Sex Secrets

The woman says:
'Oh you know. . . greeaat', but, after she has experienced the first Post-coital Huff or two (all on her own), she begins to wonder.

These are some of the things she begins to wonder:
> Has he heard from *Her*?
> Will they spend Christmas together?

The Other girls spur her on with lots of inquiries about these very subjects.

The woman reads a couple of women's magazine articles about the typical behaviour of men in a variety of circumstances in order to unearth some clues. (She reads a saucy one about SEX while she is about it.)
She's still pretty much in the dark.

In private moments the woman has something else on her mind. In private moments the woman is thinking about the events of last weekend. . .
Last weekend involved some Associated Props.

The Associated Props

- A four-poster bed (requested on reservation)
- Some massage oil (raspberry)
- Some new underwear (ruined)
- A bowl of fruit (nobody can remember)

Actually, women don't always keep this stuff private for long. Women tend to spill quite a few of the beans to other women. Men might not feel entirely comfortable if they knew just how many of the beans women spilled.

A Moving Experience

There is something that the woman doesn't mention to the other women. The magazines don't seem to mention it either. It's the Modern Woman's Dilemma.

THE DILEMMA THAT LOTS OF MODERN WOMEN HAVE

1. They have discovered that they like sex just as much as men
2. They have discovered that they know more about sex than most men
3. They consider themselves sexually liberated
4. They don't want men to think that they are Sluts

The woman does not want the man to think that she would do what she did last weekend with Just Anybody.
The woman does not want to think that the man would do what He did last weekend with Just Anybody.

Women don't always realize that men have a bit of a dilemma too.

THE DILEMMA THAT LOTS OF MODERN MEN HAVE

1. They have discovered that women like sex just as much as men
2. They worry that women might know more about sex than they do
3. They consider themselves sexually liberated
4. They wonder if a lot of these women aren't just Sluts

Sex Secrets

The man doesn't think His girlfriend is a slut. (Although, he wouldn't like to think that she'd do what she did last weekend with Just Anybody.)

The man suspects that women who come to the office in Hot-looking black outfits and read articles about SEX in the lunch hour might just be asking for it though.

One of these things happens when a relationship has reached a sexual peak.

- The man stops calling and the woman has a nervous breakdown.

In these circumstances some Really Serious bean spilling goes on. The other women waste no time in putting in their twopenny-worth.
Everyone assumes that he was hearing from *Her* all along.

- The man and the woman start planning an awful lot of weekends away.

In these circumstances people look infuriatingly grinny and glowy all the time. No one can get them to spill any beans.

- Love stuff.

In these circumstances the man:

- Feels Very good indeed. So does the woman. Christmas takes on new meaning.

When a couple are feeling Very good indeed about each other.
When Nights Alone start to feel a bit cold and lonely.
Quite often they do the Two Rooves for One swap.

A Moving Experience

Lots of women think that Living Together is the first step towards marriage.

Lots of men think that Living Together is a good way to ensure that their girlfriend isn't doing what she did a couple of weekends ago with Just Anybody.

When the man and woman start Living Together the woman is Happy and Obliging.
She is Playing House.

> **Playing House is a deep-set female thing. It has to do with teeny tiny tea sets and itty bitty cookers that really work.**
>
> **Few women can resist the urge to Play House once they get a Daddy doll of their very own.**

Women who are Playing House keep the fruit bowl in the kitchen.

When the man and woman first move in together they say things like:
'Let's not turn into a routine. Let's not always sleep on the same side of the bed.'
They have quite a lot of Nights In. They both gain a bit of weight. They watch quite a lot of TV. They always sleep on the same side of the bed.

Sometimes the couple have a silly fight but they always make up.

Sex Secrets

> ### *Silly Fights*
> Mostly, early days Silly Fights are caused by jealousy. Couples usually have someone in their partner's life of whom they are irrationally jealous.
>
> ### *The Woman:*
> Goes for someone pretty who was in the man's life BEFORE HER.
> Someone pretty who was in the man's Bed BEFORE HER is a really serious contender.
>
> ### *The Man:*
> Doesn't really think that any of the woman's previous boyfriends were very good-looking, and he avoids thinking too much about the possibility that she was in bed with anyone before him, so he isn't really too bothered by Exes.
> He is insanely jealous of some man that the woman talks about in an Admiring sort of way. Someone that the woman mentions (constantly) is Good at something (as in possibly Better than him).

At first, the man and the woman both encourage this little bit of green-eye. (After a while it is just a pain in the butt.)
At first, the Making-Up makes up for the fights.

These days the woman is much too busy for worrying and wondering much.
She spends a bit less time with the other women too.
(Women deny this but it is true.)

The man cannot imagine that he could be headed for any sort of trouble at all.

11

T.L.C.

In most relationships there is one who kisses and one who offers the cheek.
Men tend to forget that, if this cheek is in need of a shave most weekends, it is likely to come into contact with a few less kisses.

Sex doesn't desert couples just because they're keeping their knickers in adjacent drawers.
BUT couples who are sleeping together Every night sometimes do just that.
They have the odd Sexless Night:

A SEXLESS NIGHT

>   Is a week night
>   The couple have had a late supper
>   They have both had a hard day
>   The woman is pre-menstrual
>   The man wears his boxer shorts to bed
>   The woman snuggles up to the man and gives him a little unsexy kiss
>   The man gives her a little unsexy pat
>   They move apart, just a little bit, to get comfy
>   They go to sleep

Sex Secrets

The couple don't mind about the sexless nights. They're kind of cosy.
After all there is more to their relationship, nowadays, than sex.
Also, other forms of physical affection begin to develop between them.

TYPES OF PHYSICAL AFFECTION WHICH DEVELOP BETWEEN PEOPLE WHO CO-HABIT

Midweek Hi Kiss

This is the kiss that the man gives the woman in the evening. It does not involve suspension of speech by either party, usually the man is holding something – briefcase, newspaper, gear stick – when it occurs, thus precluding full embrace. Nor does it necessitate the meeting of both sets of lips.

Supper Brush

The little upper anatomy stroke that the woman gives the man when she hands him/clears away his supper plate. The woman is often on her way to the kitchen as she does this and it generally involves the meeting of her right hand and his left shoulder. Sometimes the man gives some bit of her a wee squeeze with his free hand as he reaches for the salt/remote control with the other.

Bye Bye Kissee

The woman plants this on the man's lips before she goes out shopping or aerobicing. Sometimes she has to grab his cheeks to get his attention and encourage him to pucker up properly. She says 'bye bye' and often gives him an instruction or two at the same time so a chap isn't always terribly responsive.

Neck Nuzzle

The man comes up behind the woman when she is doing something reasonably absorbing. He puts his arms around her. He gives *her* lower regions a bit of an unsubtle nudge with *his* lower regions. He kisses whichever part of her neck he can get at. Sometimes he says something incoherent at the same time.
Some women are gripped by an uncontrollable urge to finish whatever it is they are doing when this happens.

Pay Me Some Attention Pet

This is a female tactic particularly prevalent during TV sports programmes and Sunday newspaper reading. It starts out as a teasing manoeuvre but subtlety may be abandoned in favour of direct manual-genital contact if the man's response is not immediate. Complete lack of response on the part of the man often leads to a Huff or, in worst case scenarios, a Need To Talk talk. It is a bit of a cleft stick move from a man's point of view.

The Snuggle

A television and a sofa are the essential props for snuggling. The snuggle lasts until one or other party gets pins and needles in some part of them or the ads come on and the woman gets up to make a cup of tea. Both parties are shoe-less. As the relationship develops, slippers may make an appearance.

S.D.A.s

Spontaneous displays of affection occur mostly on the female-to-male axis. The woman is suddenly overcome by a sudden urge to hug and kiss the man and say something cute to him. Men love this. Sometimes they give it a whirl themselves. Unfortunately, men often misjudge the timing for an S.D.A. They try one when a woman has just spent half an hour putting her face on or when she is talking to her mother on the phone. Her response can put a man off trying it again for quite a while.

Sex Secrets

P.D.A.s

Public Displays of Affection mostly consist of hand holding and proprietorial upper thigh pats. The upper thigh pat is not specifically sexual, it is more of an unmistakable symbol of familiarity for the sake of the onlookers.

Alcohol Induced Amorousness

A.I.A. is also a public act but it is overtly sexual. Usually low lighting, loud music and best friends are party to it. It involves tongue kissing, buttock groping and lots of 'just wait till I get you home' eye-contact. If the alcohol flows much past midnight, the A.I.A. is unlikely to be the prelude to a private performance. Sometimes women see this as a bit of a breach of promise and a Huff ensues. The man doesn't notice.

The couple settle into a bit of a routine:
One (maybe two) weekday, not-too-energetic, 'Oh-go-on-put-it-in-then' liaisons.
Once (maybe twice) monthly a little Saturday night black stocking/tie-me-up, tie-me-down adventure.
Plus fairly regular, pre-breakfast Sunday morning dalliances which begin rather more slowly than they finish.

Life *could* go on, quite happily, like this for ages . . .

12

He Had It Coming

Sometimes a woman gets together with a man she loves very much. She cooks for him, buys him little treats, gives him a back rub if he is feeling poorly, does his washing for him and hangs up his clothes. She reminds him about little things that he might forget and always remembers to buy razors, vests and socks when he needs new ones. She takes very good care of him. Just like Mama did.
The man loves this.

After a bit the man goes out and finds someone who wants to play Doctors and Nurses with him.

Women like a relationship to be Going Somewhere.
This means that even when things seem perfectly OK, they'd quite like Something to change.
Men don't Understand this.

> Lots of men would be happy for the relationship to stay pretty much as it was on the third date . . . FOR EVER.

After she has Played House for a bit the woman would like some Appreciation for her efforts. Also, things have been the Same for ages.

Sex Secrets

The woman finds herself feeling a wee bit Resentful because the man:

'Isn't Making Any Effort'

As a rule men don't notice any of this.
If they do they ignore it.
The couple have entered the Foreplay War Zone.

SOME EXAMPLES OF BEHAVIOUR WHICH MIGHT LAUNCH A MAN INTO THE FOREPLAY WAR ZONE. *FAST*.

  1 Absolutely Point-blank Refusing to go to the supermarket with the woman in his life
  2 Finally agreeing to go to the supermarket with the woman in his life and Then. . .

- Throwing a wobbly about the lack of parking
- Throwing a wobbly about the lack of trolleys
- Filling trolley with ice cream, baked beans and some bottles of Bulgarian plonk (which a smiley girl is giving out samples of) and Then. . . Throwing a wobbly because the woman in his life isn't ready to go home yet.

The man knows that Something is Up because the Terms of Endearment, which have worked like little charms so far, seem to have lost their magic.

One night the woman is feeling very upset about the man's lack of effort.
She is upset because he doesn't seem to want to Discuss anything about their relationship.
She is a bit sniffy about something he said at breakfast too actually.

He Had It Coming

The woman gets into bed and moves Right to the Edge.
She has her back to the man.
She sighs a bit.

The man rolls towards her and begins a lazy, but fairly specific sort of one-handed fondle.

The woman feels upset and angry.
She thinks: 'How can he think I'd want to make love to him after what he said this morning?'
She Stiffens and Removes the man's hand.
She figures he will Get The Message.
(She thinks they can have a Proper Discussion i.e a Need to Talk talk, about a few things that Need to Change, tomorrow.)

The man feels as though a rock just fell on him.
He thinks: 'She doesn't fancy me any more.'
He does Not feel like Discussing ANYTHING.

Couples who are living in The Foreplay War Zone find that their Silly Fights start turning into Very Big fights indeed.
People who are having Very Big Fights have them about almost anything.
The only thing that the couple living in the Foreplay War Zone Don't fight about is sex.

NOT TALKING ABOUT SEX IN GENERAL. SOME REASONS FOR. . .

Women don't because they

a) Feel a bit embarrassed
b) Are scared that men will think they're Sluts if they make a Specific Request
c) Suspect that asking a man to do something that he is not Already doing might make him feel inadequate.

Sex Secrets

Men don't because they

a) Feel a bit embarrassed
b) Are scared that women will accuse them of treating them like Sluts if they make a Specific Request
c) Would feel Really Inadequate if the woman asked them to do something they weren't Already doing.

In general people rely on Hints and OOH AAAGH noises. People with flatmates have terrific collections of stories about this.

In the Foreplay War Zone the couple start having Very Big Fights because someone says:

'You KNOW I don't like cooked tomatoes.'

After a bit people get really fed up with fighting. Sometimes they break up. Sometimes they sort things out with a spot of Wooing. Sometimes they just watch a lot more TV.

> If you asked 200 couples which they would prefer to give up for six months, Sex or TV, a lot of them would hesitate.
> A lot of them wouldn't.

The couple begin to dress in a watching-the-TV sort of way.

The icy strip in the bed thaws a bit, in its place there's a Tepid Divide across which hands or feet might stray, familiar and heat-seeking.

Lust's fervent flame does Not project the flickering shadows of love on to the blind.

He Had It Coming

The woman thinks:
Maybe I should consider (she means Threaten) leaving, If we're not going to get married.

The man thinks:
There's no point in leaving unless (he means Until) I meet someone I want to marry.

Quite a few women don't Really want to marry the man they live with.
Most women convince themselves that they do. There are two reasons for this:

- They consider that a Proposal is a really major bit of Wooing.
- They cannot Face being in anything Remotely resembling a 'Where *AM* I?' situation Ever Again.

Quite a few men Don't leave, even if they Do meet someone they want to marry. Some men (more than women like to think) pretty much Get Married to this someone and Then leave. In these circumstances the woman has a chance to experience life on the other side of the Overlap.

A couple can cohabit in The Foreplay War Zone for an age.
Unless . . . one of them hears the Beat of Jungle Drums.

13

Missing Kinks

'And he'd run after me and grab me and kiss me. Hard. I'd resist him...'

'And she'd be BEGGING for it...'

People are Unfaithful for all sorts of reasons.

SOME REASONS THAT MEN ARE UNFAITHFUL

Sometimes a chap is having a spot of bother with one woman. (Another one helps to take his mind off things for a bit)

Sometimes a chap feels lonely

Sometimes a chap feels unappreciated at home

Sometimes a chap is having a crisis. (Chap's crises are Usually to do with Power or Money)

Sometimes a chap wants to recover his lost youth

Sometimes a chap feels under pressure from the other chaps

Sometimes a chap just had the chance

Sometimes a chap's wife gets a bit sloppy about her appearance

Sometimes a chap has had one too many

Sometimes a chap thinks that he's God's gift to women and monogamy is for the birds

Missing Kinks

Women are Unfaithful for lots of the same reasons but there are differences.

A DIFFERENCE

Women always Say that they were Unfaithful because the man in their life wasn't treating them right, i.e. they weren't getting enough Wooing.

A BIG DIFFERENCE

Lots of women spend lots of their Possibly Being Unfaithful years having babies.

Stolen moments are Not high on the agenda of people who are: Exhausted and/or Carrying an extra ten to thirty pounds.

During the gestation and early infancy of these babies many men are particularly vulnerable to Overlap Opportunities.

Some men
> develop an Out of Town habit at this stage (these men figure that 'One Time Only's when they're away from home Don't Count as infidelities).

Some men
> find an Overlap Opportunity has moved right into the house. (This O.O. speaks with a foreign accent. She is very good with the baby.)

Some men
> meet a savvy, sassy, smart woman during this period of their lives. They respond to the beat of Jungle Drums. This sort of behaviour can lead to heartbreak and revenge-seeking of unbelievable proportions.

Sex Secrets

Unmarried women are slightly less likely than married ones, or men, to actively Look for Trouble.
Usually, for a while at least, they cling vainly to the hope that Marriage might put things right.

Women can get so caught up looking for Love that Lust goes right out the window.

Occasionally, when a woman is in a 'What the Hell?' sort of mood, she says to another woman (who is definitely a Good Sort):

> 'He's very supportive and kind and sweet with kids and doing well in his career and Nice and has a Sense of Humour and he really is Good at lots of things and I do LOVE him . . . but . . . '

After this ' . . . but . . . ' she says something which implies that This man, whom she Loves, is Not a Passion.
She says something which implies that someone else Was.

Women who are in a dangerously 'What the Hell?' mood say something which implies that someone else IS.

Women end up with men that they Just Don't Fancy more often than they want to admit.
Women often say that The Foreplay War Zone and Tepid Bed Syndrome are the direct result of Men's Failings, i.e. not enough Wooing.
But the truth is:

Some men could go to the supermarket until they were blue in the face and still find themselves feeling fairly Unwanted in the Underwear department.

Missing Kinks

When a woman Loves a man but Just Doesn't Fancy Him

She says:
- 'That's all right love, you go without me.'
- 'No, no, stay up and watch it. I want an early night.'
- 'I've got a *meeting* in the morning.'

Sometimes the chap on the receiving end of this behaviour feels that he is being Rationed.
Sometimes he is.

This chap does one of these things:
- Runs up his Visa Card bill shelling out on a load of stuff that might get the woman in the Maybe Mood
- Eats a lot, works a lot, drinks a lot, watches a lot of TV

Often, he comes to the conclusion that monogamy is for the birds.

When a man Loves a woman but Just Doesn't Lust After Her

He does this:
- Eats a lot, works a lot, drinks a lot, watches a lot of TV.
- Takes to watching women in a way that implies more than Idle Curiosity.

Often, he runs up his Visa Card bill shelling out on a load of stuff that he keeps in the shed. The woman would have some pretty Concrete Evidence, re. his sources of pleasure, if she ever stumbled in there.

Men don't have heart to hearts about this sort of thing with the other fellows.
Instead they have a few drinks and then one of them says:
'What's the connection? Chinese food and . . .'

Sex Secrets

He doesn't need to finish. The other men shout:
'You don't get either of them at *HOME.*'
People who settle down together are liable to forget something; it's this:
Men and Women don't come in kit sets
A person cannot find another person who is a perfect match.
A person cannot get another person with All the optional extras.

Fortunately, the bit that is missing often has to do with towels on the bathroom floor
Unfortunately, the bit that is missing often has to do with something more intimate.

This stuff makes for a complicated cocktail.
If lots of Ice is added to this cocktail, bedrooms get glacial.

A taste of Hot Toddy is terribly tempting when you're suffering from hypothermia.

14

Playing Away

*'I don't know, it's a fishing trip or something . . .
just think, I used to go With him to things like that.'*

'I'm going to be back late tonight.'
'Uh-huh.'

TWO STORIES

First Story

One Friday a man is asked if he'd like to join a group of the lads who are going to an out-of-town game. He says 'yes' immediately. He has a bit of a think; he thinks:
'This is really going to send her off the deep end, I'd better call her.'
He calls the woman in his life. He says:
'Hiii, sweetie.'
The woman is a bit taken aback because he hasn't gooey called her for a while. She feels the old warm fuzzies rising to the surface.
'Hiii,' she says. She is a bit cautious.
'Sweetie, look, some of the other chaps are off to the match this weekend, and um, . . . they've got an extra ticket and you know . . . they said do I want to go.'

Sex Secrets

The woman closes her eyes. She feels quite upset inside, she feels a fight coming on. She says:
'So you're going?'
(She says this in a frosty dentist receptionist type tone.)
The man says:
'Look if you're going to make a BIG DEAL out of this I'll just forget it . . . OK, Just Forget it.'
The woman says nothing for a moment. She wonders what is happening to them.
She thinks: maybe a couple of days apart wouldn't be such a bad thing.
She says (in as sweet a voice as she can manage):
'No that's all right, darling, you go. You'll enjoy it.'

On Saturday, when the men are on the way up the M1, they are all in high spirits.
They tell the odd crude story, they talk in a way that they don't talk when there are women about.

> Men sometimes find it easier to Talk to each other in cars because they don't have to Look at each other at the same time.

After a bit they pull over at the service station. The man goes to pee.
When he gets back he is surprised to see two blonde girls in jeans putting back-packs into the boot.
The man feels a bit pissed off. He wonders who is going to sit where.

One of the girls sits in the front. The other one sits in the back between the man and the other chap.

Playing Away

The chap who is driving puts a tape on, he grins at the woman next to him and starts drumming on the steering wheel like a lunatic.

The man feels Really pissed off. He feels that the weekend has been Tainted.

The girl next to him notices that he is a bit tense. She says:

'Are you OK?'

'Hunh?'

'Are you OK?'

As the girl says this she tucks her hair behind her ear and smiles a lovely smile. Then she twiddles a bit with the safety belt.

The man's recall of what happened between this moment and the moment when he looked up to see a blonde girl standing in front of him, wearing nothing but a pair of high-cut knickers, is a bit hazy.

The man's recall of the soft little golden thigh hairs which these knickers revealed is not at all hazy.

The man remembers thinking at the time that he had never seen anything so lovely as those soft little golden thigh hairs.

He has thought this quite a few times since.

Second Story

One day a woman is asked by her immediate boss to attend a meeting with a chap from the marketing department.

When they get to the meeting the chap from the marketing department doesn't look all that thrilled to see her there. He seems pretty pissed off, actually.

The woman and her immediate boss listen to the marketing department man's ideas.

The woman's immediate boss doesn't seem too enthusiastic about these ideas. She says something like:

'I don't really see my role in this.'

The man looks *really* pissed off. He looks as if he is about to lose it. Then the woman says something.

Sex Secrets

This something implies that

- She understands the ideas
- She likes them

This something is Savvy, Sassy and Smart.
The man sits up in his chair. He looks at her in a way that implies slightly more than Idle Curiosity.
The man and woman have lunch together.
The man tells the woman how much he Appreciated her comments at the meeting.
The woman looks up at him from under her eyelashes.
The man tells the woman a fabulously amusing anecdote about her immediate boss.
The woman finds herself smiling an awful lot.

When the man suggests a drink some evening she tucks her hair behind her ear and says:

>   'Well, maybe . . . '

That evening, when she is chopping carrots and the man in her life is watching the news, she thinks:
'What the Hell?'

```
Boom  *  Boom  *  Boom  *  Boom  *
Boom  *  Boom  *  Boom  *  Boom  *
```

Jungle Drums can get fairly Loud. Sometimes people start tapping their feet to the beat. They go off exploring. This is what they discover:
Sex which takes place

- In secret
- In confined surroundings
- Instead of lunch

is likely to be of the heated sort.

Playing Away

People who are doing it Anytime and Anywhere:
People who are doing it with complete disregard for the consequences: Don't have any doubts about how much they fancy each other.

> They don't have time for dinner at Luigi's
> They don't have time for Post-coital Huffs
> They Never get to spend Christmas together
> They get straight to the point

Specific Requests are not just alluded to. Specific Requests are often discussed.
These discussions really Pump Up The Volume.

15

You'll Pay For This

'Yes, but I mean it's only complete perverts who go to these girls, foreigners mostly, I should think . . . and the odd poor fellow who is just so lonely and unattractive that no normal woman would look at him.'

Some people don't hang about waiting for Trouble to come and get them.
Some people go On the Hunt when the Home Fires aren't burning.

In general these people are men.

All sorts of men go Honey Hunting seriously.

BUT:
Generally, men cannot rely on Getting Lucky

AND:
Not many men can make grown women swoon

ALSO:
Most men figure out, fairly speedily, that no amount of aftershave or breath freshener is going to change this fact.
Quite a lot of men decide that spending money on drinks for giggling girls who won't come across is a waste of time.
Quite a lot of men decide that if they're going to spend money, they'd rather spend it on a Sure Thing.

Except for those women for whom Love is Just a Job, most people try to ignore this fact.

There are women who Don't associate Lust With Love.
There are women who Understand a lot more than other women do about Specific Requests.
Some of these women dress in the traditional style of streetwalkers and then proceed to actually walk the streets.
They don't usually walk them for long enough to catch cold.

Some of these women dress in the traditional style of Very Contented wives. They never walk the streets, in fact they are driven pretty much anywhere that they want to go.
They do the same job.

Most people try to ignore this fact.

Men visit prostitutes, or ladies who don't pay rent, for all the same reasons that men are Unfaithful generally.
Plus the whole problem of being:
b) scared that women will accuse them of treating them like Sluts if they make a Specific Request
goes away when wallets enter the proceedings.

Lots of women are touchingly naive about men's Specific Sexual Requests.

73

Sex Secrets

> It simply would not occur to most women that a man might fantasize about someone because of the way that her Mouth moves when she talks.

Mostly a modern woman catches on to the Mouth Moving thing once it is pointed out to her. She rolls her eyes and laughs and says:

'Oh, *that*.'

The look on her face implies that this Request is sometimes made at home.
The look on her face implies that this Request is not always satisfied willingly.

Lots of women think that Specific Sexual Requests are Always something to do with the way that women look.
A modern woman says:
'Well, you know, I wouldn't mind. . . dressing up a bit.'
When a woman says this she means that she wouldn't mind wearing something that she thought she looked pretty Hot in.
She would expect a man to –
not only, Appreciate this
but also, Tell her that she looked pretty Hot
(It goes without saying that *SHE'D* be wearing the rubber miniskirt.)

Sexually liberated women think that what people do in the privacy of their bedrooms is their own affair. They say:
'If people want to dress in rubber and tie each other up, that's *their* business.'
Sexually liberated women aren't averse to a bit of tying up themselves.
That is, if they're with their One and Only, who they Trust not to Hurt them.

You'll Pay For This

Only One doesn't do it for some men.
Some men want a little hurting.
Some men want someone to hurt Them.
Some men want a whole bunch of stuff having to do with bodily functions that most people don't think of as sexy At All.

These men seek solace in the arms of women who never ask: 'What are you thinking?'

ONE MORE THING

Gals who Work It for a serious living know how to make a man feel very Adequate indeed.

ONE MORE, ONE MORE THING

When a woman has Gone Off it, she usually figures she's Gone Off it. Sometimes some bits of a man Go Off it all by themselves.

Sometimes a man has a spot of bother with a Flat Battery.
Lots of women don't mind about this much. Especially if they like the starter and the pudding course best.
The man minds very much indeed.
If the Flat Battery goes on for a bit, and the minding very much indeed begins to interfere with the starter and pudding course, a woman may do a bit of reading up on the subject. (In her heart of hearts a woman is a bit concerned that a Flat Battery might be her fault.)
A woman may also try a few tricks that she hasn't bothered with since her Wooing days.
Sometimes this works. Sometimes it doesn't.
Sometimes, a man with a Flat Battery goes out in search of a Magic Vag.
This search takes a lot less time if he Hunts for Sure Things.

Sex Secrets

The man thinks that if he could just find the Magic Vag, and feel Adequate again, everything would get kick started back into life.

Too many disappointments in the search for the Magic Vag can be the cause of a completely dead engine.

❧

The hours, expense and financial outlay that Honey Hunting involves can cause men to develop a haunted look deep in their eyes.
(Some of them look remarkably Unhaunted, actually.)
If a man does develop a Haunted Look the woman in his life Ignores it.
Sometimes one of the woman's friends suspects that she detects it.
The man in the life of this friend keeps his mouth shut.

> Men can be pretty much One Hundred Per Cent relied upon to keep their mouths shut about another chap's little peccadilloes.
> If a man bumps into another man who is very obviously Out of Bounds, the Out of Bounds man is not usually kept awake by the fear that this man might have a word with his wife.
>
> An Out of Bounds man who bumps into someone else's wife knows that there is a very good chance that he is
> 3   Heading for Deep Trouble

Lots and lots and lots of men say:
'*I've* never had to pay for it in my life.'

Some of these men haven't had a very close look at their Visa Card bill lately.

16

Something's Up

'Where did you get this shirt?'
'Who was that on the phone?'
'How could you lose your wedding ring?'
'Why are you taking a shower?'
'Who did you see it with?'
'Why would I want to go alone?'
'What have you done to your hair?'
'When were you in York?'
'What was Carol getting at?'
'Can't someone else work late?'
'Won't any of the wives be going?'
'What's that mark on your neck?'
'Whose hairbrush is this?'
'What does it say on that matchbox?'
'Have you changed the sheets?'
'JOGGING, since when?'
'What's this receipt for?'
'Where were you when I called?'
'Why won't you come to bed?'
'Who's it from?'
'What's this phone number?'
'Is that perfume new?
'Why are you so touchy lately?'

'Of course the Spouse is always the Last to know'

Sex Secrets

When someone in a Living With or Married To situation IS feeling a bit Haunted, Everyone gets caught in the Tension Trap.

THINGS THAT PEOPLE WHO ARE SEEING SOMEONE ELSE AND FEELING HAUNTED DO WHEN THEY'RE AT HOME

> Bellow or Screech a lot
> Feel guilty and act a bit gooey
> Bellow or Screech again
> Lie
> Go all quiet
> Keep going all quiet
> Say (in a bellowing or screeching kind of way): 'You KNOW I don't like cooked tomatoes.'

The other person behaves like you'd expect someone to behave if they had a sound like a car alarm going off in their head twenty-four hours a day.
This ringing isn't always imaginary.
Occasionally, the person who the person is seeing Phones Home.

Frostbite sets in.

Outside Interests can have another side effect . . .

One day a woman detects an itch. She ignores it for a day or two.
She takes plenty of showers and figures it will ease.
It doesn't.
She buys some vaguely medicinal cream and tolerates the scrutiny of the pharmacist. She thinks the cream will fix it.
It doesn't.
After a few days of this the woman makes an appointment.
As she walks through the door of a clinic with grim linoleum and nasty orange chairs, she plasters a confident look on her face.
This look is meant to say: 'It's only Thrush.'

Something's Up

No woman who is attending the Wednesday evening clap clinic ever believes that anyone else there has Only got Thrush. She thinks twice about going to the loo.

The woman's name is called by a tired nurse with an 'I know . . . it's ONLY Thrush' expression, and she is ushered in to see the doctor.
The doctor looks at the woman's itchy bits, asks her a lot of questions about them (to which she gives non-specific responses) and then says:
 'How many sexual partners have you had in the last year?'
The woman is Very specific:
 'One.'
It is at this point that the doctor begins to look sympathetic and explain about it NOT being Thrush.

By the time the woman has picked up her prescription she is feeling Very Upset Indeed.

All women say that Under These Circumstances they would go right home and Hurl the nasty little plastic container right between the eyes of the man responsible. (These eyes would look pretty damned Haunted as a result.)
Under These Circumstances quite a lot of women Would do just that.
Quite a lot of women wouldn't.
Women don't Always confront men when they have Concrete Evidence of infidelity. As a general rule these women fall into the Unmarried and In Love category. Insecure is a pretty prominent feature too.

Some of these women are able to convince themselves that S.T.D. stands for:
*S*omething *T*o *D*o with washing powder/the Pill/nylon knickers.

79

Sex Secrets

Women don't usually tell Clap Clinic stories, they just can't see the funny side.
Men do. Men's Clap Clinic stories are usually combined with a 'Who was *SHE*?' story. They always end with the man saying:
'I swear, I thought it was going to DROP OFF.'

If the woman who visited the clinic is in a Living With or Married To situation:
If the woman who visited the clinic HAS had More than One sexual partner in the recent past:
She is likely to be feeling more than Haunted by the time she gets home.
She is likely to be suffering from the worst bout of Morning After Sickness that she has ever known.

Sometimes Morning After Sickness has long-term side effects . . .

Every now and then a woman, who is feeling really desperate in the Tension Trap, decides that a Baby might make things all right . . .
Women with babies on the brain can often manage to warm up a bedroom for just long enough to stir up a whole heap of trouble . . .

'But you KNEW I was going off the Pill.'

Another Bit on the Side effect . . .

Sometimes a man is having an affair because he thinks that the woman in his life doesn't Fancy him anymore. This man would quite like to convince the woman in his life that he is actually the

Somethings Up

World's Greatest Lover. He sets about trying to convince himself, and the woman he is seeing, that he is the World's Greatest Love He thinks that the woman in his life might catch on by some sort of osmosis.

She Doesn't.

Alarm Bells and Jungle Drums *fortissimo*.

There are some animals who will gnaw off their own legs rather than remain caught in a trap.

There are some people who can sympathize with this reaction.

17

Knock It Off

A woman gets up in the morning,
Puts a load of washing on;
Pays the newspaper bill on her way to work;
Makes a quick call to book the holiday;
Ducks out at lunchtime to get a few groceries;
Books the car in for a service;
Rings the man to tell him that she has booked the holiday and the car in for its service;
Calls the couple they are having dinner with on Saturday to check what time they should arrive;
Stops by the locksmiths on the way home to get some keys cut for the new cleaning woman;
Waters the pot plants;
Takes the washing out and sorts it;
Hangs up the jacket that the man wore yesterday;
Puts the supper on.

When they sit down to eat the man asks her if she had
a chance to get his mother a birthday card.

Sometimes a man and a woman don't do too much messing about.
Sometimes a man and a woman just get married.

Knock It Off

This man and woman sort of go together, like a horse and carriage.
They Can't imagine Not having their knickers in adjacent drawers.
They are awfully content. The love action between them is pretty much of the Old Magic Variety.

When the Old Magic starts up, in a friendly kind of way, on a Saturday Night, the woman thinks:
'Aaaah yes, this is how we do it.'

BUT. . .

Sometimes even Very contented couples, who love each other, find themselves with a spot of Tepid Bed Syndrome.
Passion becomes a bit of a hazy memory, actually.
They don't put Very much energy into doing anything about this.

One reason that they Don't

Well, there are so many more Important things, aren't there?

Some more reasons that they Don't

- Kids
- Just Tooo Tiredness

These two things are often connected, although Corporate Couples are prone to the same malady.
When the J.T.T. Couple hit the sack, their minds are heavily geared towards Getting Horizontal. And staying that way.

Sex Secrets

BEHAVIOUR PATTERNS OF PEOPLE WHO ARE J.T.T.

Falling asleep on the sofa
Falling asleep on the sofa with the TV on
Falling asleep on the sofa with the TV on, and a newspaper over their faces
Falling asleep on the sofa with the TV on, and a newspaper over their faces, while three kids and a very frightened dog play inter-galactic space wars in the next room

---

KIDS PLAYING INTER-GALACTIC SPACE WARS

When two kids (your own), and one of unknown origin, shut themselves and the hapless hound in the dining room with various long sharp things and the odd tea towel (for tying around their heads), life can get very noisy indeed.

The male way
to deal with this situation is to ignore it completely unless actual blood begins to seep under the door.

The female way
to deal with this situation is to Try to ignore it for a bit and then, when either
    The noise reaches screaming pitch
or
    It stops altogether (As in 'It's too quiet in there')
go rushing in with the intention of rescuing the dog or that other kid from some hideous fate.

Knock It Off

Sometimes a man who is asleep on the sofa with the TV on and a newspaper over his face gets woken up by the terrified yelps of the dog or the other kid, and, because he has had a Tough Week at the office and could REALLY do WITHOUT this, he yells (in his Big Daddy voice) for his wife to do SOMETHING about those kids. He reminds her that he has told them, not once but a hundred times, to let the dog Out of the damned house.

The woman who hears this yell emanating from the sitting room, while she is sorting washing, is likely to go right off the deep end.

She yells back. She yells about why doesn't Mr High-and-Mighty get off his butt. Does it look like she's got nothing to do?

The man reacts to this by hurling the newspaper off his face and STORMING into the dining room. (He has his Big Daddy face on.)

HE SHOUTS at the people who are in there (all these people are under four feet tall) and he is none too sweet to the dog.

Silence.

The kids and the dog slope off to the other kid's house.

The man goes into the kitchen and takes a beer out of the fridge.

His wife says: 'Well, that was reeaally helpful wasn't it?'

The man says: 'Look I'm just Toooo tired for this, ALL RIGHT?'

His wife says: 'Oh . . . and *I'M* not, I suppose?'

That's all they say. It's enough.

The Old Magic loses a wee bit of its lustre.

Later on, when the kids have dragged themselves back from the other kid's house, and they've eaten their tea and had their bath, the woman tells them it's time for bed.

The girl one says, will Daddy read them a story?

The woman sighs and says that Daddy is a bit tired. As she says this a look of disappointment crosses her children's faces to accuse her.

Sex Secrets

She takes this accusation downstairs to her husband who is watching the news.
She says: 'They want you to read them a story.'
The accusation in her voice irritates the man, he is about to give vent to his irritation when he looks up at his wife and sees the tiredness in her eyes.
He feels a bit guilty.
He says: 'All right, just give me a minute, OK?'
The truth is that the man doesn't really mind reading a story to his children. He loves them very much. It's just that:
Well, There are so many more Important things aren't there?
The man climbs the stairs and goes into his children's room. (The boy one is holding the Rupert the Bear book.)
The man takes the Rupert the Bear book and says:
'All right, tiger?' to his son.
He smiles a weary smile at his little princess and starts to read the story.
He is just beginning to relax when the girl says:
'Trudy's getting a divorce.'
The man stops reading and looks at his daughter for a second.
She looks up at him.
'Trudy, in my class . . . that I go to swimming with. She's getting a divorce and her Daddy doesn't live with her any more.'
The man gives his daughter a little hug. He figures there is no particular question to be answered so he continues with the story.
When it is finished he gives his kids a kiss and switches off the light.

He has two options.

One of them is to go into the kitchen and stand there in the dark, looking out at the back garden for a very long time.
If a man doesn't take this option. If a man goes back to his very tired wife and gives her a little kiss on the top of her head, and suggests an early night, the Old Magic might put a bit of a sparkle back into her eyes.

Knock It Off

In the morning she might look a wee bit grinny and glowy when she fixes the kids their breakfast.

A smart man might do a little Wooing and throw in a few Terms of Endearment.
A smart woman would smile an awful lot at this man.

A Really smart couple would do some of this In Front Of The Children.

18

Sweaty Palms

Mosquitos never feature in people's Outdoor Fantasies.

Often, when couples decide to give Wooing another whirl they figure that a bit of a Thaw is called for. They go Somewhere Hot.

Most people imagine that going Somewhere Hot will change an awful lot of things.
Most people imagine going Somewhere Hot will have a spectacular effect on their sex lives.

> A woman who is planning on a Passionate two weeks wearing Next to Nothing packs forty-seven co-ordinating outfits and some extra gold sandals, just in case.

Once the couple have decided to go Somewhere Hot, the woman:

> Tells at least one other woman about this plan. (Possibly tells several other women about this plan.) Spends a lot of time deciding What to Pack. (Discusses this with the other

Sweaty Palms

women.) Does something to her hair. Decides she isn't sure about what she's done to her hair. (Discusses this with the other women.) Has a person who dresses like a dentist, and inflicts about twice as much pain, do things to the hair on the rest of her. Buys some new kind of cream which makes thighs thin. Goes on some kind of thigh-thinning diet. Buys something which she saw in a magazine article called *Bare Essentials*. Buys a new bikini. Has a last-minute change of heart about What to Pack.

If a couple are going Somewhere Hot because the Woman has had an affair, she doesn't do any of this.

Men never do any of this.

When the couple get Somewhere Hot the woman changes into her first co-ordinating outfit. She does this as soon as they have been shown up to their room and she has had a bit of a shufti at the bathroom and the balcony.
The man gets changed too. He is a bit quicker than the woman. He waits for her on the balcony.
They decide 'What the Hell?' and they order a drink. They have it on the balcony.

While they are having a drink . . .

The Man
Tells one of his stories.

If Somebody has had an affair, the man figures that this will ease the intensity of the atmosphere. If Nobody has had an affair, he tells it out of pure *joie de vivre*.

Sex Secrets

The Woman
Laughs in all the Right Places. She twiddles a bit with the stem of her glass.

> If the man has had an affair, the woman can only keep this up for the first day. After that she thinks: He'd probably rather be with *Her*.
>
> She behaves like a person who has a car alarm going off in her head.
>
> Too much of this behaviour is liable to convince a man that he'd rather be with *Her*.

When they have had their drink. . .

The Man
Says 'Ready to go then?'

The Woman
Says 'Just a tick'. She goes to the bathroom to pee.
She does a bit of a 'What do I look like?' inspection while she's about it.

When they get to the Al Fresco Restaurant. . .

The Man
Says, 'What do you think about this lamb?'

The Woman
Says, 'Lovely, and look they've got that Chianti we like.'

> If the man has had an affair the woman says: 'You KNOW you don't like lamb.'
>
> Then she says:
> 'Or is that something else I've got wrong?'

Sweaty Palms

When they've had their supper...

The Man
Says 'Ready to go then?'

The Woman
Nods, then she smiles.

They walk the long way back to their room. The man puts his arm around the woman's waist. They don't say much. They feel awfully good on account of the warm night air and the Chianti and the arm around the waist.

When they get to their door...

The Man
Takes his arm away from the woman's waist. He puts the key in the lock and then he turns around and kisses her. Right there on the landing.

The Woman
Kisses him back. Eventually she pulls away, but she keeps hold of the man's hand. She tucks her hair behind her ear with her other hand and she looks up at him from under her eyelashes.

When they close their door...

The Man
Kisses the woman again.
Next thing they are on the bed, half undressed, making love.
When it is over they are both a bit glowy. They look into each other's eyes. They start grinning like mad.
This couple spend the next two weeks Bonking like Billy-ho.

Sex Secrets

> If the man has had an affair, this doesn't happen because the woman cannot get That Slut off her mind for long enough.
> If the woman has had an affair, this doesn't happen because the man is feeling Inadequate.

COUPLES WHO GO SOMEWHERE HOT AND DO BONK LIKE BILLY-HO, REASONS FOR

- No vests
- No kids (Kids who go on holiday with couples generally get sent somewhere with grim linoleum and nasty plastic chairs, for Fun Times in the afternoons)
- Alcohol in the afternoons
- Dirty Books

When couples go Somewhere Hot. They buy lots of Big Books to take with them.
Women buy books with SEX on every third page.
Men buy books with EXPLOSIONS on every third page.
They have the same effect.

Some couples who go Somewhere Hot are Not actually a Couple. (Say no more.)
Before they go on this holiday, these people say things like this to Other people:
'You KNOW how difficult it is to get to a phone at these conferences.'
This couple does Not go home sporting a tan.
This couple orders dinner in their room.
(The woman still packs forty-seven co-ordinating outfits and some extra gold sandals . . . just in case.)
There are people who go Somewhere Hot with the specific Intention of finding someone to Bonk like Billy-ho with.

Women with B.L.B. on their minds

Pack EIGHTY-seven co-ordinating outfits and more gold sandals than you can imagine. They spend a lot of time letting Totally Unfanciable men buy drinks for them so that they can Flirt Madly with the waiter.

Men with B.L.B. on their minds

Start out smelling of aftershave. Pretty soon they just smell of beer.

Sometimes a couple go Somewhere Hot. Nobody has had an Affair.
Nobody feels like Bonking at all.

Even in Very Hot Places indeed, beds can remain Tepid.

Sometimes a couple find that with:

- No kids
- No gas man
- No work

to talk about, they really haven't got very much in common.

In these circumstances a woman is liable to realize that worrying about Hair and What to Wear was a bit of a waste of time.
The man hasn't noticed any of it.

Couples who've rediscovered each other's ticklish bits keep glowing for a fair while after their tans have faded.
In the middle of winter they have a jolly good evening at Luigi's poring over holiday brochures.

Sex Secrets

The woman finds herself wandering wistfully into Resort Wear on more than one occasion.

Couples who've discovered that Nothing gets them giggling anymore aren't holding hands when they get off the plane.
They stand stiff as stalagmites at the luggage carousel.
Not much later they do the One Roof for Two swap.

Women who've been fun-hunting in the sun come back with Fabulous tans. (Even if it is the middle of winter they wear Resort Wear for weeks afterwards to show it off.)
Men who've been hoping to Get Lucky with a fun-in-the-sun huntress come back with hangovers.
Sometimes, these men and women rediscover their ticklish bits when they get home. These ticklish bits are downright itchy.
Doctors and nurses have a huge collection of stories about this.

19

Different Strokes

'... Don't STOP'

The thing is, a person can develop an Itch which has absolutely nothing to do with anything Nasty.

Sometimes, when a woman is all grown up.
When a woman has played at Playing House and Love Stuff for quite a while, she starts to hanker after a spot of Lust.
Quite often the woman comes to this conclusion just as her man is thinking:
'What the Hell? If she wants me to go to the supermarket, I'll Go to the supermarket.'
Everybody is confused.

When Swooning replaces Wooing in a woman's wish list she doesn't do much about it at first.
Well, there are so many more Important things aren't there?
Also,
A woman who has got

- A nice house to play in
- A nice man in her life (who is fanciable with a sense of humour)
- An annual Hot Holiday (with some OK bonking thrown in)
- AND maybe a cute Kid or Cat or two

Sex Secrets

Doesn't like to complain.

Still, the Itch is there. She can't scratch it.
Often, even when a woman has a pretty clear idea of how she could Get Some Satisfaction, she keeps it under her hat.
This has nothing to do with b) Anyone thinking she is a Slut.
It's just become a habit. She's got so used to thinking:

> 'This is how we do it.'

Something that Women Keep Under Their Hats . . .

Lots of women would like the man in their life to be a little more Masterful, in the physical department, occasionally.

As a general rule, the only men who are seriously Masterful are:
    a)   Slimeballs from hell
    b)   Men who've been recently cuckolded
    c)   Men who are paying for it

Most other men are:
- Too nice
- Too lazy
- Too tired
to try it.

One day one of the woman's friends says something like:
> 'Maggie is getting married again and we're having an Anne Summers party'
> 'The badminton crowd have organized a night at the Chippendales'
> 'There's a season of French Films starting on Sunday. Would you like to go?'

If the woman follows up one of these invites.
If the woman finds herself in a situation where Lust is being discussed openly.

She might just go home and show the man in her life what Masterful is all about.

This man might find that even the supermarket has a Saucy Side . . .

'Whipped Cream, Darling?'

If a man is suffering from nothing more than a spot of rust in the Old Magic department, whipped cream might make a remarkably effective lubricant.
Quite a lot of men, though, just like things to stay as they are . . . For Ever.
A man who is trying to watch the news isn't always terribly responsive when a woman (whom he's hardly said a word to all year) comes rushing in, grinning and glowing like mad, and starts talking saucy.
This woman is faced with a battery which no amount of jumping is going to start.
She breaks out in Prickly Heat.

SEEN TOO . . .

One summer's evening a man is on his way home. He has had a few drinks. He is feeling pretty good, on account of the drinks and the warm night air. A pretty girl stands next to him at the lights and he smiles at her. When she smiles back he feels absolutely full to the brim with *joie de vivre*.
Now, this man always walks to the train by the same route. It is not surprising that he has noticed a rather saucy looking knicker shop next to the station. Mostly he has had no difficulty putting this to the back of his mind.
This evening though, what with the warm night air and the few drinks and the *joie de vivre* the man has a thought. It is a thought about a weekend a long, long time ago. The man is still thinking this thought when he finds himself paying the gift-wrapping girl rather a lot of money for rather a small parcel.

Sex Secrets

A bit later on this man is feeling as if a rock fell on him.
The word Slut is ringing in his ears.
He has a few more drinks.

Flirting Madly takes on a whole new intensity for people who are feeling Itchy. People who are feeling Itchy, who have had a few drinks, get into some Really Intense Flirting.

Really Intense Flirting usually involves at least one of the following:

- A lot more drinks than is good for anyone
- Christmas
- A soon to be ex employee
- Someone else's current spouse
- A mini cab

After an Intense Flirting (plus a few drinks) session people say:
'I didn't *mean* anything by it.'
They say this to:
    The cab driver
    The girl's mother
    Somebody else's spouse
    Their own spouse
    The flash lawyer with the charge of Sexual Harassment
    The flash lawyer who they've gone to, to file a charge of Statutory Rape

Most people who Flirt Madly don't want to Leave the Nest. They just want a window on the outside world. Some people skate dangerously close to this window.

Couples who are feeling Itchy and Not Mentioning it look at other couples and Wonder.

Actually, couples look at other couples and wonder all the time.

Different Strokes

It doesn't matter how much wondering goes on though, most people don't know the half of it.

Sometimes a man and a woman really Get It On.
    They have a chemical attraction.
    They have an Entire Matching Set of pheromones.
    These two like to do a little Thrill Seeking in the privacy of their own home.
    (Their next-door neighbour's home and a club where you have to ring the door bell three times might be on their itinerary too.)

This is a couple who are into Specific Requests.
Some of these requests are Very Specific indeed.

In Modern relationships the V.S.R. trail often starts with a V.C.R.

If a woman has got a video camera And a man in bed with her (let alone the next-door neighbours), she is likely to be Extremely concerned about What She Looks Like.
She has a little discussion about this with her man.
She and the man go on a little outing.
They go to a shop with blacked-out windows.

If this man and woman have still got kids in their nest, they have some Very Strict Rules about KNOCKING.

A man and a woman who have a whole lot going on, in terms of Human Union, have a sort of bond.
This bond makes Public Displays of Affection unnecessary.
This bond is visible between the unlikeliest of people, when they look into each other's eyes.

Sex Secrets

Actually, this same kind of bond is apparent between people who go on ballroom dancing courses, or hill walking holidays in the Dales together, so it isn't always a surefire giveaway.

Sometimes a woman is all grown up and Single.
Mostly she is happy that way.
She goes on some jolly nice holidays and she buys whatever *she* wants at the supermarket.
If you asked her, she'd say that she'd rather have Wine than Wooing these days.
Still . . . sometimes . . . the nights alone feel a bit Cold and Lonely.

If this woman

   a)   Likes sex
   b)   Knows a bit about sex
   c)   Doesn't give a fig what anyone thinks of her

She might just get herself a toy with batteries included.
A Boy.
A lot of Good Times can be had in an arrangement like this.
BUT, if the Boy has Brains and is Nice, with a Sense of Humour –
Even a very grown up woman indeed can find a little Morning After Sickness sneaking up on her.